LEARN TO ADAPT, ADAPT TO LEARN

CONFESSIONS OF A KINDERGARTEN TEACHER DURING THE COVID-19 PANDEMIC

GRETCHEN POLENZANI

CONTENTS

Dedicated to
The 2020–2021 MES kindergarten team…
True pandemic warriors!
And
My husband, Joe (Mr. P), who helped me survive the most
stressful year of my career.

PROLOGUE: A TALE TO TELL
DECEMBER 2020

While attending our kindergarten team meeting and listening to the team as we shared our hilarious accounts of remote teaching five-year-olds, the superintendent turned to me and chuckled. "When this is all over, you should write a book."

"It" is far from over, but this is my story, and this is that book.

POLENZANI... OUT! (MIC DROP)

DECEMBER 2018

I don't remember exactly when colleagues and parents began inquiring about my retirement, but over the past few years, it had started coming up more and more.

Teachers who had been hired in the same year as me were asking, "How much longer before *you* put in?"

Families that I had known for years, whose kids I had all taught, were saying things like, "I hope you're still here when this last one of ours comes to kindergarten." (The last one in question still currently in his momma's belly.)

My standard reply had been to laugh. "Oh, they'll probably have to carry me out of here in a bag!"

Truth be told, I was starting to actually imagine a life

after teaching. I was ready to relax, to sleep in every day, maybe to do some traveling, pursue some hobbies.

I was living vicariously through retired colleagues on Facebook.

Our current teacher contract would be a good contract to "go out" under, as the negotiated benefits for retirement were pretty favorable. You never knew what you were going to get in the next contract—maybe fewer salary bumps, maybe none. Maybe health insurance for a limited time, maybe none at all.

Besides, twenty-plus years of teaching kindergarten —constantly on my feet or sitting on itty-bitty chairs and criss-cross applesauce on the carpet—were taking their toll. It was getting harder to get up off the floor once I was down there! Frankly, I was tired, and all the "why"s were becoming more tedious with each passing year.

"Why do I have to wear my coat?"

"Why can't my snack have peanut butter?"

"Why do I have to write with a pencil?"

"Why does she get to go with a special teacher and I don't?"

"Why can't I wear these flip-flops for Gym?"

"Why do you have a tattoo?"

"Why is your finger bloody?" *(a teeny tiny hangnail barely visible to the naked eye)*

Why, why, why!

Lately, it had been all I could do not to snap, "Because I said so!"

So, after much thought and careful consideration, I submitted my letter of Intent to Retire from Teaching to the district superintendent and Board of Education.

My letter was accepted, and I was officially in the retirement "pipeline"; my salary for my last six years would be cemented in place with percentage "bumps" as laid out in the teacher contract. I would be finished in June 2024. I only had to teach six more years to be fully vested and receive a really good pension. And once I was in the pipeline, I couldn't get out of it unless I had a life-altering experience, like the death of a spouse or a divorce. (Global pandemics, I would come to learn, didn't count.)

Big whooshing breath. *Done.* No turning back. I was more than okay with it; I was relieved, ecstatic! It was a light shining at the end of what would be thirty-five years in the classroom, most of them in kindergarten.

Yes! I could begin purging my bulging files and my rafts of personal teaching supplies that I'd collected over the years, a passage I'd enviously witnessed many colleagues going through in previous years. And if you know a teacher (or are married to one), especially a kindergarten teacher, you know that we are hoarders. A cabinet full of paper towel tubes, egg cartons, baby food jars, and plastic water bottles? You never know when those will come in handy for a science experiment! Bins overflowing with random craft items—paper bags, glitter, felt, cotton balls, buttons, and sequins? Just when you get rid of them, you'll need them for a Mother's Day project or an impromptu "Get Well" card for a classmate. Fun foam, pipe cleaners, googly eyes in every size...? Well, you get the idea. It would take me every bit of six years to go through it all.

Time to think about life after teaching.

Time to coast on out.

Ah, but it was not meant to be. School year 2020–21, The Year of Pandemic Teaching, would find me working harder than I ever had (no coasting here) in a brand-new arena where I did not feel particularly comfortable. It was to be a constantly challenging learning curve, one that often left me feeling like a first-year teacher, reduced to tears, and kept me stressed out and exhausted 24/7. I would find myself adding to my files (especially my digital files) at a rapid rate, as the kindergarten team was adding many new and different lessons to accommodate the shift to digital and socially distanced learning. Purging would vanish entirely from my mind.

SICK MUCH?

JANUARY/FEBRUARY 2020

2020 started off rough at school, especially in kindergarten. So many sick kiddos—an unprecedented number. Weeks and weeks were missed due to fever and flu symptoms, though the kids were negative for Influenza A and B. There were seven cases of pneumonia in my class alone. And the lingering coughing! (As long as kids were fever-free, they could be in school.) It sounded like a TB hospital whenever one walked down the kindergarten hallway.

I think I had nine students absent on Valentine's Day.

I was very ill myself over the President's Day weekend. I'd had a flu shot the previous October, so I couldn't believe I was so sick. I remember thinking, "If this is the flu, it's kicking my butt." I had major digestive issues and ran a fever of 102 for a few days. It took over a week for me to get back to feeling normal. Thinking back to that, it certainly makes me wonder... could my symptoms have pointed to something other than a typical gastric virus?

It was about this time that the news was ramping up with reports about a newly identified virus in China. I remember thinking, "How bizarre" when I saw a clip on the nightly news of people in China going about their everyday business wearing masks, but I am ashamed to admit that I really didn't pay close attention. There was a brief flicker of alarm in my brain, and then I remembered the SARS scare and the MRSA panic and the H1N1 flu. Here, and then... mercifully gone.

IT HAS A NAME

MARCH 2020

Now the novel coronavirus, SARS-CoV-2 (dubbed COVID-19), positively dominated the news. Apparently it was here in the US, and probably had been for a while. People were becoming infected at an alarming rate, especially on the coasts. Travel was being discouraged. Several of my students were upset that their spring break plans were being ruined by the "stupid co-ro-no-vi-rus." (To hear that rolling off the tongue of a five-year-old, each syllable carefully pronounced!) Others reported that their dads and/or moms weren't going to work anymore. Phrases like "flattening the curve" and "social distancing" were being tossed around between teachers in the hallway and workroom.

The district superintendent, Dr. Jason Lind, called a

staff meeting in the first week of March; his serious manner was alarming. Never had I seen our staff so quiet and attentive. When I think back to that meeting, there were well over fifty people gathered together. Right after that, the governor of Illinois recommended no gatherings of more than fifty, then twenty-five. Like dominoes falling, the new edict of "social distancing" caused the cancellation of school sports, clubs, after-school care, and field trips.

Dr. Lind maintained that we would stay open for classes, enforcing distance as best we could. Cleaning and disinfecting would be increased within the school building. Spring break was just two weeks away.

A *big* focus on handwashing and hand sanitizing began. We taught the kids handwashing tips (like singing "Happy Birthday" three times, ensuring that the recommended twenty seconds of scrubbing time was accomplished), which made for a perpetually long line outside our classroom bathroom.

"I sang it ten times, Mrs. P! My hands are super clean!"

My aide and I disinfected tables and shared supplies daily, wiping down pencils and glue sticks and scissors.

Kindergartners can and do put inappropriate things in their mouths on a daily basis (and yes, some do eat glue). Disinfecting wipes were flying off the shelves, at school and in stores.

One week later, on Friday, March 13, 2020, at 1:30 p.m., we were alerted via school email that we were shutting down at the end of the day, as per the governor's executive order, until after spring break at the earliest. Since spring break did not begin until March 20th, this meant that we still had a week of class to teach—and we would be teaching it remotely.

Mad scramble! Get the iPads and chargers into the backpacks! Get some leveled readers into the folders! Make sure the students take home their Phonics and Handwriting workbooks!

According to Dr. Lind, the pressure had been building to close schools that week. The Lake County superintendents were unanimously in favor prior to the official announcement. As Dr. Lind half-jokingly recalled, "When the NBA suspended play, I knew it was very serious."

Teachers huddled in the hallway, trying not to panic. All of us shared the same thought: surely we'd be back after spring break, once this virus settled down (and went away)... right?

It is rather interesting to note: that particular week in March 2020 involved a time change, a full moon, Friday the 13th, COVID-19 soaring toward pandemic status, and a national emergency (lockdown). Just sayin'.

We were instructed not to say anything to the kids— let their parents handle how to tell them what was happening and why. We sang our goodbye song, and they finished triumphantly, "See you on... Monday!"

I was fighting back tears. They had no idea. It was eerily similar to 9/11, when the world changed in a single morning, never to be the same. When I put my kindergartners on the buses that afternoon, I made sure to hug each one tightly (social distancing be damned!). Little did I know that I would not see them in person again for the remainder of the school year.

4

WHAT IN THE WORLD IS HAPPENING HERE?

APRIL 2020

"Anthony Fauci" and "social distancing" became household terms, along with "Personal Protective Equipment" (or "PPE")—gowns, masks, gloves. What was happening was so unbelievable that we adults could not tear ourselves away from CNN's constant virus updates: the drama, the horror stories in New York, the lack of hospital beds, the bodies lining hospital corridors.

That caused ever-present anxiety. "What if I get it? Or my children do? Or my elderly parents?"

How could anyone actually believe contracting this illness was similar to catching a cold or the flu? How could people be so uninformed? Even more unbelievable to me was that some people thought the whole thing was a hoax, an idea that was being perpetrated by our very own government. (Pretty elaborate hoax, if you ask me.)

More COVID-19 symptoms were added to the growing list every week—"YOU MAY HAVE COVID-19 IF YOU HAVE [fill in the blank]." Therefore, each little sneeze or headache caused paranoia. Everyone I know thought they probably had "the COVID" at one point or another that spring. Our hands were red, raw, and cracked from constant washing and sanitizing, mine to the point of bleeding.

We all became obsessed with sanitizing. At our house, my husband Joe and I were constantly wiping down counters, fixtures, doorknobs, TV remotes, even our cell phones. We would wipe down the groceries after bringing them home and before putting them away.

I was trying to conserve our supply of paper towels and was washing hand towels constantly. It was thought at the time that the virus was not only spread through the air, but also through touching items that may be contaminated.

When the president declared during a press conference that we'd "all be together in church on Easter Sunday" with this "China Flu" mostly under control, I didn't know whether to scoff or weep at the ludicrousness of that notion. I'm pretty sure I did both.

At that point, mask-wearing was advised only for

people with COVID symptoms. This was due mostly to the fact that there was a national shortage of PPE, and frontline workers were woefully undersupplied.

But then the thinking abruptly changed, like it has done several times throughout this ordeal as more knowledge has been gained about how the virus spreads. Masks became more readily available. Soon we found ourselves ordering a package of one hundred disposable medical masks (at ridiculously inflated online prices).

"This virus will be long gone before we'll ever use all of these," I remember telling my husband. Who could've guessed we'd be out of masks (and buying more) by midsummer? Who would've thought that, one year later, face masks would be a fashion statement (one I grudgingly got sucked into) and sold anywhere from convenience stores to high-end department stores?

I rummaged through my linen closet and turned up a box of disposable gloves, using them when I went to the grocery store or pumped gas, only to quickly find out that that was a no-no, probably spreading even more germs. But it ended up making perfect sense that gloves were a no-no, especially when food shopping: pick up an orange with gloves on, decide not to buy it, then move on to the tomatoes and squeeze a few, and the whole time you're potentially transferring the virus as you go. Right? We still used gloves when we got gas, disposing of them after. But really, fill-ups were few and far between—we weren't going anywhere.

As luck would have it, Joe had done his monthly Sam's Club run a week prior to the lockdown. We had an abundance of Clorox wipes, toilet paper, and paper towels. This turned out to be perfect timing; soon it was impossible to find hand sanitizer, paper towels, or toilet paper in any store. Meat cases at the stores were empty for those first few weeks, too. Then flour and yeast disappeared from shelves. People were hoarding (and apparently baking a lot of bread).

Challenging times. Unprecedented times.

It all turned bad so quickly.

Teaching and learning were flipped on their ears. Basically, life as we knew it had shut down. With everyone in quarantine, we teachers were forced to deliver instruction virtually after spring break. If someone had told me ten (or even five) years ago that one day I'd be teaching from my kitchen via computer, I would've laughed in their face.

It helped then, as it helps now, that we are very blessed in our school community; all of our students have a school-issued device and almost all have easy access to the internet.

That spring, teaching was mostly asynchronous (a term that would become a buzzword in education):

lessons were planned and posted online with little live interaction. Students logged on and followed the lesson plans provided by their teachers.

These lessons were *very* meticulously planned virtually by my whole kindergarten team through the Zoom app. *Hours* of Zoom meetings. Using our laptops, we could all be on the editable lesson plan document at the same time, while searching ideas on Seesaw via our iPads, while texting on our phones. Kindergarten teachers are, by nature, masters at multi-tasking, and that served us very well.

Luckily, our K team—five of us then—got along well. We had, and still have, a mutual respect for what each of us brings to the team. (Being the senior member, my contributions have nothing to do with technology. I know enough to get by at school but still often struggle with the three TV remotes at home.)

Our goal was to keep our students engaged and on track. We followed our spring themes as best we could. Unfortunately, spring is when we cover many of our Science Core Standards, and thus instruction includes a lot of hands-on activities. This year there would be no planting seeds and watching our garden grow on the classroom windowsill. No growing butterflies and releasing them on a sunny spring day. We wouldn't be able to make a Water Cycle in a Bottle or a Cloud in a

Cup. The students would miss out on creating shade structures outside with recyclable items for our experiment on temperature.

Also, because the students were now seriously lacking in pencil/paper work and other small motor tasks like coloring, cutting, and manipulating Play-Doh, I began to worry about how much their handwriting would regress. (Sorry, first-grade teachers!) But, as our administration pointed out again and again, to us and to families: *we were in the middle of a pandemic* (for at that point, that is what it had indeed become). What we were doing was being referred to as "Crisis Teaching." In survival mode, we were all doing our best to just get by.

It was amazing how much there was for me to learn about apps like Seesaw, Epic, IXL, and Reading A-Z, the apps we relied so much on now that we could not be in person for lessons. Of course, our kindergartners were exposed to and used to logging into these apps (and many others), but never had we leaned so heavily on virtual assistance to teach concepts, provide review, and practice skills.

I had been using Seesaw in the past, but only as a way to communicate with parents, posting weekly updates and photos. Now it became our primary vehicle for assignments. Through Seesaw, I was able to virtually check the students' work, comment, and/or send it back to them for corrections. Reading A-Z allowed me to log in every day and listen to recordings of my students reading leveled books. Who knew? The IXL app was great for reinforcing reading and math skills, allowing each student to work on individualized goals. And I was able to make book/video collections on Epic for the kids, encompassing spring themes like plants, the water cycle, and insects.

I took to posting a twice-weekly Story Time video, my daughter Lizzie wielding the camera (she and I had so much fun!). The kids always looked forward to those. I dragged home big books, puppets, and anchor charts from my classroom. I appeared in bunny ears to read a story about spring. I dressed up as Mother Goose to read nursery rhymes. I dug through my daughter's plastic tote of Beanie Babies to present a lesson on oviparous animals ("Which one does not belong?"). I actually went through my kitchen waste bins on camera, sorting trash and recyclables for Earth Day.

Essentially, I was "teaching" from my kitchen—or sometimes the dining room, or the family room, depending on how much I needed to spread out. Charts were hanging from the fireplace mantle. Notebooks and binders were piled on the kitchen counter. My school world and home world became hopelessly blurred.

God bless the parents that spring. They were thrust

into being teachers, basically. Some were more natural at that than others. While they could be counted upon to see that their children logged on and completed their assignments (well, most of them), following the lesson plan turned out to be a bigger ask. Some parents seemed to think it was like a pick-and-choose thing, especially during those first few weeks.

There were a couple of kids in my class who were conspicuously "not present" much. (Oh yes, we had to keep track—we had a weekly checklist, recording which apps each child was on and how often.) I couldn't be judgmental; the kids' lives were in upheaval too. Parents were juggling their own crazy, just like me.

My laptop would start blowing up with emails at precisely 8 a.m. Every. Single. Day.

"We can't log on."

"What's the password for _____?" *(Did you check the list I sent out—twice?)*

"Your link isn't working."

"Does my daughter need to complete _____? She doesn't want to."

"My child doesn't understand what to do with _____." *(That activity is for Friday and this is Tuesday. Please follow the lesson plan.)*

"The iPad won't stay charged." *(Fill out a tech support*

ticket online. Someone from the Tech department will contact you.)

"We have finished everything for the week. Can you send supplemental work?" *(Um, it's Monday. What??)*

"We can't find that app." *(Did you watch the tutorial video I sent that shows you exactly how to find it and load it?)*

"My son is fighting me and won't do any work." *(I was fighting my husband and didn't want to do any work either. I'm positive he was tired of my constantly whining, "I CAN'T DO THIS!")*

But I had it easy compared to some colleagues. At least my kids were grown. I could not fathom having a baby, or a toddler—or, God forbid, school-age children! —and trying to manage all of this. Many teachers were juggling their e-teaching and their own kids' e-learning.

All I had to worry about was my husband and daughter, one furloughed and one working mostly from home. One morning they decided to make fruit smoothies… with a Ninja blender… in the kitchen… during my Zoom meeting. *Really?!* My husband, Joe, popped into the frame with me. He had a pretty good COVID beard going, and it was predominantly gray.

"Hi, kids! How's it going?"

"Is that your dad?" the kids asked.

I remember seeing a meme around this time: ONE DOES NOT SIMPLY TELL KINDERGARTNERS TO

LOG IN. If I wasn't so stressed, I probably would've found that funny. But joking aside, five- and six-year-old children are *not* independent. They need an adult close by, at the very least in another room. It's very hard for them to stay focused and follow directions when left to their own devices on Zoom. They will unmute themselves and start calling out randomly to classmates, completely overriding whatever I am saying. They will start fiddling with whatever toys are within their reach. One girl completely undressed her Barbie doll for all to witness.

And the issues and questions from parents persisted all day, often into the evening hours. I was aware that some kids did their schoolwork in the evenings and/or on weekends due to circumstances in their households: Grandma was in charge, but didn't know how to navigate the internet. Mom/Dad needed to attend their own meetings and conference calls during school hours; there was no one to supervise their child's e-learning. Some kids were at the *one* childcare center that was still open in our area; their parents were essential workers and clearly not available to help them. *Nothing* was getting done at daycare; it was way too chaotic. One child had no internet access and his mom was having him use a hotspot, which was eating up too much data on her phone.

What was I supposed to do?? I needed to be available, but was desperate for some downtime away from my laptop, iPad, and iPhone. When should we be able to unplug for the day? Should I be obligated to check school email on the weekend? Some parents were floundering; I felt that I needed to offer advice whenever I could and at least be there to listen.

Every teacher, at my school and probably across the country, was grappling with these issues.

But overall, I have to say that parents were very grateful and did not hesitate to reach out with questions (or, on occasion, advice!). I think they truly appreciated our efforts. I know I truly appreciated theirs.

I vaguely knew about Zoom prior to this time. Now it began to run my life. Meetings that we would have attended in person had school been "open" found a way to go on as usual. It amazed me how quickly we as educators learned to problem-solve and adapt. Staff meetings, committee meetings, team meetings, IEP meetings, and on and on. I had four to five Zoom meetings every day. It was exhausting.

Although we were not required to Zoom with our classes at that time, it was encouraged. I was nervous to explore that option, but began hosting three to four Zoom meetings a week to see my kids "live" and give them an opportunity to see and talk with each other. I was concerned for their social and emotional well-being. (@#$%, I was concerned for my own.)

I tried to keep our meetings interesting and light, always asking, "What's new?"

"Does anyone have a new baby at their house? A new pet?"

"Who has lost a tooth?"

"Are you being good to your mommies and daddies?"

We had virtual show-and-tell and scavenger hunts.

"Find an example of a cube."

"Look in your fridge and see if you have a root vegetable."

"Bring back a sphere."

"Can you find something around your house that is living? Non-living?"

"Ready, go!"

I really missed my students.

But those early Zooms were stressful and chaotic. I had knots in my stomach before and during. I still did not trust my technological prowess at all. I was learning at a fast rate; it was sink or swim. And there were a lot of fails. I was struggling with Speaker view versus Gallery view. Sometimes I would end the meetings accidentally. One time, I locked a kid out and couldn't figure out how to allow him back in. I did not like looking at myself on the screen. It was a hot mess.

There were funny things too, which we would vent about and laugh about in our weekly team meetings. It was a wonderful way to relieve the pressure and to each know that we weren't navigating these uncharted waters alone.

Picture this:

A child with an iPad, camera on and running at full speed down a hallway: "Come and see my bedroom!" (Or my closet, or my toys!)

"I have to go poop!" (Or get a Pop-Tart, or let the dog out!)

[TV blaring in the background.]

[Baby screaming in the background.]

[Parents arguing off camera.]

[An occasional F-bomb being dropped off camera.]

[Pets of all kinds coming to kindergarten.]

The mute button became my best friend.

My cat, Gizmo, became an unlikely star of our Zoom one day when he leaped onto the counter to stand on my keyboard (his way of asking for attention, of course). It's all the kids could focus on, the cat's butt, never mind what I was saying. In every meeting thereafter, they asked for Gizmo.

I dressed professionally every day (at least on the top), did my hair and make-up, and wore earrings. It helped untangle the lines between work and home. I was never one of those teachers who could wear pajamas, *not* shower, or *not* put on mascara.

Presenting myself as "put together" was a way to keep from falling apart. (Until late May, when I hosted our last meetings from my bed, wearing my glasses and certainly no lipstick.) *"Mrs. P, are you wearing your pajamas?!"* At that point I was running on empty and was past caring.

In late April, the decision was made to continue remotely for the rest of the school year. The students' supplies and belongings had to be packed up and delivered to them. A plan was developed for teachers of each grade level to come in on a certain day—the goal was to minimize having too many bodies in the building at once —pack up the items (masked and wearing gloves, of course) in clear trash bags, and place them in the hallways outside the classrooms. The bags would be organized onto buses by route number and delivered to each home in the district. God bless all of the paraprofessionals, bus drivers, teachers, and administrators who signed up to facilitate the process. I couldn't; I just didn't have it in me.

Walking into the school was eerie; it was like entering a time capsule. Hanging from the ceiling in the kindergarten hallway were shamrocks and leprechauns. My classroom seemed frozen in time as well. On the whiteboard was the date MARCH 13, 2020, written in green marker. I will never forget that date. March rainbows made out of paper plates were suspended from the ceiling. The students' little gym shoes and the random items like forgotten mittens and hoodies in their cubbies broke my heart.

My aide and I packed all the bags as instructed and placed them out for pickup. It was a sad sight, all those bags lining the hallway. I was going to cry… *again*. How I hated that this was going to be the way the year ended for these kindergartners! No Spring Fling, no Kindergarten Picnic. Well, at least not one case of COVID-19 had been reported in our district (contrary to what was to come). We had apparently done the right thing by shutting down.

5

TEACHER LOVE

MAY 2020

S igns were delivered to every teacher's yard by our school board members for National Teacher Appreciation Week. They read "WE LOVE OUR TEACHERS" with the district logo. I proudly displayed that sign for seven months, until it was time to decorate for Christmas. It's still in my garage; I don't think I could bear to get rid of it. (The hoarder in me?)

Administrators and teachers organized a parade for the first week in May. It was held in the parking lot of a local mall. We teachers came, parked our vehicles (spaced out in every other spot), and stood at the ready in our school spirit wear. Yes, it was May, but although the sky was a brilliant blue and the sun was shining, it was *cold* (maybe thirty degrees Fahrenheit) with a whipping wind.

We all wore masks that had been specially ordered in our school colors: "MILLBURN MATTERS." Most of us had made signs to hold up as the parents drove their kids up and down the rows. "MISS YOU!" "HANG IN THERE!" "YOU ARE SUPERSTARS!" "YOU ROCK!"

Students waved signs as well. "LOVE AND MISS YOU!" "[insert teacher name here] IS THE BEST!" "THANK YOU, TEACHERS!"

It was heartwarming and just the boost everyone needed. Every single one of my students came by that day. I wanted to jump into their cars and hug them all (even the ones who had pretty much been the bane of my existence). I was alternating between laughing and giving air hugs and... dissolving into tears. What a strange time indeed.

At the end of May, we went around and personally said goodbye to our kindergartners. Little district buses took each teacher and aide to our students' houses. We stood six feet apart on driveways and on porches, delivering report cards and end-of-the-year gifts (a Millburn Mustang lunch bag and water bottle, bubble wands, and sidewalk chalk—things usually given out at the Kindergarten Picnic).

How to manage report cards had been the subject of much debate that spring. I was a member of the report card committee, and kindergarten had just rolled out their new standards-based report card in the fall. It was the pilot for all of our elementary grades as we worked toward alignment with the national Common Core standards. It was a pivotal move away from letter grades—focus was on Mastery (of the standards). Marks were given according to a specific rubric.

There was no way, given the current situation, that we could do the assessing that was necessary to complete that report. Similar circumstances were reported across grades one through five, even though the other grades had not yet converted over to standards-based assessment.

Ultimately, for all students at the elementary building, T3 (Trimester 3) was changed to "RL" (Remote Learning) and *everyone* was given a "P" (Pass) in the "Comment" section.

"P" = The Student Has Provided Sufficient Evidence for Passing during Remote Learning

I had a couple of students who absolutely had *not* provided evidence anywhere near sufficient. Many teachers had students who did next to nothing during this remote-learning period. But ISBE (the Illinois State Board of Education) was recommending a "do no harm" policy; focus should not be on grades. ISBE was cautioning us not to give failing marks, citing that it wasn't fair to punish kids who had little to no access to the internet (the great Digital Divide). That wasn't an issue in our district, but we did as we were told.

Teachers added comments specific to each student. I wrote "I AM SO PROUD OF YOU!" many, many times during that grading session.

It was so hard not to give or receive hugs during that last goodbye! The kids seemed taller and were starting to resemble true first graders. I had expected that the kids would be a little shy, but some were simply struck mute that their teacher was standing in their front yard!

One thing I truly did *not* expect were the many parents who came out on their driveways to say "thank you." Many of them had bouquets of flowers and other gifts for us. My favorite was a ceramic decorative plate, clearly hand-painted: "AS THE WORLD STAYED APART, OUR CLASS STAYED TOGETHER, MRS P" plus each child's name, lots of colorful hearts, and of course, "2019–2020." The experiences that day provided much-needed closure but were emotionally draining. I have never, ever been so glad to see a school year end.

Kindergartners' Belongings Packed up and Ready for Delivery (4/2020)

My First "Fancy Mask," Made by a Friend (4/2020)

Teacher Appreciation (5/2020)

Special Thank-You Gift from a Kindergarten Family
(5/2020)

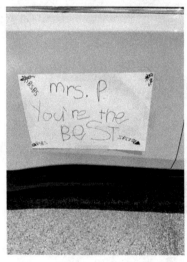

The Millburn Parade at Gurnee Mills (5/2020)

Homemade Pasta! (6/2020)

6

THE WEEKEND
JUNE/JULY 2020

Being a teacher, I always think of summer as a weekend: June is Friday, July is Saturday, and August is Sunday.

With the arrival of June (Friday—yippee!), I put my laptop and iPad into my schoolbag and let the batteries go dead. I began seeing my chiropractor twice weekly (she said I was a mess). My eyes were suffering from so much screen time that I was prescribed drops and an updated contact prescription.

I slept a lot during that first month of summer break. I'm pretty sure I was suffering from what was a brand-new phenomenon, pandemic fatigue. I did not want to think about anything, especially if it was school-related. In the back of my mind, I thought—as did most of my colleagues—that it would be great to get back to "normal" (teaching) in the fall. But I would think about that later.

Restrictions had been lifted a bit, and at least we could be outdoors now, as the weather was pleasant and mild (contrary to the typically fickle midwestern spring, which had brought snow in April).

That helped. Joe and I spent a lot of time sitting on the front porch, walking in the neighborhood, or on the trail in the forest preserve nearby. We had a small personal "bubble" of friends we spent time with that summer, grilling out together or enjoying occasional outdoor dining, which so many local restaurants were offering. We were doing a fair amount of cooking, exper- imenting with homemade pasta (who had had time for that in the "old days," as we were calling them now?). We ordered takeout at least once a week, trying to support local businesses. We always had a jigsaw puzzle going on the dining room table. We finished a couple 500-piece ones and, feeling over-confident, moved up to a 1000-piece (mistake!).

Blessedly, we were able to see our children regularly. Our daughter Lizzie was living at home then, and our son Eddie was nearby in an apartment. They spent a lot of time with us (well, Lizzie was sort of stuck with us). I think being together in their comfort zone helped the kids deal with those uncertain and scary days. Back in their childhood bedrooms, Mom making dinner, having the family together playing Scrabble, watching old movies. When a crisis occurs, all you want is your family tight around you. It was soothing for Joe and me, too.

I was feeling less anxious, especially as COVID positivity rates began to go down...

... and then came July.

July (Saturday) was full of angst, like those Saturdays when you are frantically rushing around trying to complete everything on your chore list.

Right after the July 4th weekend, school supplies began appearing in stores, as is typical. Ads on television touting online ordering and curbside pickup began focusing on "the new school year, whatever it will look like." The return to school was all of a sudden in my face and on my mind. Talk was circulating amongst my team and colleagues: would we return in person? That thought terrified me. I just could not fathom how the schools could be made safe enough. Teaching while masked? Enforcing distancing with five-year-olds? No shared supplies or toys in kindergarten? No recess, no lunchroom? Ever-constant sanitizing?

But on the flipside, how on earth could you begin a new school year completely remote? Your students wouldn't know you; their parents wouldn't know you. How could you take on a class of fresh kindergartners during a pandemic, when they are so dependent and helpless (even in a normal year)? An integral part of kindergarten is the social/emotional learning that takes place: how to make friends, how to get along in a group, how to share and problem-solve. How could that be taught and practiced through a computer? Additionally, the incoming Kinders were at a distinct disadvantage in that they did not have a chance to even finish preschool due to the spring lockdown. How could you correct a pencil grip through a screen?

At least last March, when the world stopped, my students and I had had a relationship. They had had relationships with each other. We had been three-quarters of the way through the school year, and they had had a solid base of reading strategies and sight words. I had known their learning styles and how to manage their behaviors. They had refined their small motor skills—coloring, cutting, writing (holding a pencil properly, for goodness' sake!). They had been learning their way around their iPads—literally—recognizing them as learning tools, not just something to play on.

With my first glimpse of backpacks and notebooks in the Target aisle, as if everything was normal, those thoughts never left my mind. I had headaches and crying jags. One weekend, I could not even leave the couch. While I had slept through much of June, July brought many sleepless nights. I had thrown myself into a tizzy reading (probably too many) articles online. One particular article that kept me up at night was written by a COVID-19 frontline nurse who was electing to keep her own children home from school. She spoke of throwing teachers into the proverbial lion's den. "Teachers will die," she predicted. Exposure = risk. How could we ask teachers, who have been cautiously isolating for months, to come back to school and expose themselves—and their families—to potentially hundreds of outside contacts?

I wished I could retire right then. It crossed my mind more than a few times.

I just had to express my concerns—they were eating me alive—so I submitted a letter to the Board of Education, to be read at the July meeting.

July 8, 2020

Message to the BOE

This statement is a personal one, and not necessarily reflective of the opinions of my team or other colleagues at Millburn 24.

I AM AWARE.

I am aware of what President Trump, Education Secretary Betsy DeVoss, IL Gov.

Pritzker, and even the Academy of Pediatrics is recommending. I am aware that parents pay my salary and want their children back in class and back to a somewhat normal routine. They believe that having children in the classroom is vital to students' social and emotional health, and I wholeheartedly agree with that!

In-person learning is essential for teachers as well. There is nothing that we want more than to be back with our kids. I am also aware that the virus is still very much in our midst, lurking.

"Get the students back to in-person learning." But at what risk? Just how much actual learning is going to be taking place? Will it be worth it? *Any* plan to reopen can look viable on paper, but execution of a plan, in my opinion, will be difficult —if not impossible.

Returning to school, whatever that looks like, will expose staff to hundreds of children and potentially thousands of household contacts.

EXPOSURE = RISK.

Your reopening plan must surely include hiring additional cleaning staff to keep up. Teachers cannot be expected to execute that feat!

IMAGINE: trying to physically distance twenty —or even ten—kindergartners.

IMAGINE: teaching while masked and taking care that students all keep their masks on properly and sanitize appropriately.

Effective teaching and class management require *proximity*. I foresee a management nightmare.

IMAGINE: packing away all the manipulatives, toys, and books because students can't share anything. Introducing the iPads immediately, even though it is developmentally inappropriate—but we have to prep the students for the remote learning that is sure to come.

IMAGINE: getting down the hallway (if just to the bus). It will be a logistical nightmare. A class of twenty, properly distanced, would be a line 120 feet long. Your reopening plan will surely include hiring additional support staff to effectively manage just moving through the hallways.

IMAGINE: a child throws up or wets his pants. What to do? Take him to the nurse? But wait, there are a couple of kids with possible COVID in there, waiting for their parents to pick them up. And the nurse is dispensing meds for another student, while checking on a diabetic child's blood sugar. Quite certainly, your reopening plan will include hiring additional nurses?

I think that what works for the upper grades just isn't viable for early childhood, unless additional safeguards are put into place. "The devil is in the details," and the details right now are quite overwhelming.

I guess I am asking, can we guarantee the safety of our school community if we return to full-on school? Will the quality of learning taking place under such stressful circumstances be worth the risk?

Do I think remote teaching children—especially our youngest learners—is the best solution? Absolutely not. It is far from ideal. But we are blessed in this community because our kids *all have access to a device.* I'm just going to leave that there. That is a whole other issue for another day.

GLOOM AND DOOM? OR REALITY CHECK?

Whatever plan the district puts forward, know that your teachers will undoubtedly and wholeheartedly rise to the challenge to the best of their ability. That is what we do.

But take care that you are not asking the impossible.

There were strong (and emotional) opinions and arguments on both sides, in favor of going back in person and against it. On the national scene, our president and the US Secretary of Education seemed to see no problem with opening schools in the fall ("Kids need to be in school!"). But they blithely skimmed over who would pay for it—air filters, partitions, PPE, additional staff to reduce class size, etcetera. At that time, there was no offer of federal or state funding to help with reopening costs. Many districts immediately shut down even the possibility of opening in the fall; they could not afford it.

Reopening plans would differ between districts, counties, and states. In Illinois, the decision was being left up to individual school districts, with guidelines set forth by the CDC and ISBE. LCHD, the Lake County Health Department, also weighed in.

Large and powerful teachers' unions across the country were indignant at the thought of sending their people back into classrooms. Our union, MFT (Millburn Federation of Teachers) was diligently monitoring the process and making sure our teachers were protected.

The majority of our certified staff wanted to come back in person, while about one-fourth did not. Those who did not were directed to take full remote positions, one at each grade level (based on a survey of staff).

There was to be much shifting around of positions, too. Our entire intervention team would be disbanded and put into classroom homeroom positions, something they hadn't done for years.

The term "hybrid learning" came into play at this time. Basically, "hybrid" covers all that lands between in-person and remote. It could involve students coming into the school building so many days per week on a rotation schedule and doing the rest of their learning online, or it could mean teaching with some students in class with the teacher and some at home Zooming in, specifically referred to as "blended" learning.

What?? You have got to be kidding me.

I. Could. Not. Even. Imagine.

What would our reopening plan be? Dr. Lind was waffling, as he would later admit. It was a delicate balance trying to appease the board (they were split), staff (not all wanted to come back in person), and parents (the majority wanted an in-person reopening).

It was a tough position to be in. Relying heavily on the ever-changing COVID-19 data points (mainly positivity rates) in our community, Dr. Lind took the decision very seriously.

As he later explained, "It was a life-or-death decision, a huge weight to bear. On one hand, if you don't open schools, kids will die (anxiety, depression, possible suicide in older kids). On the other hand, if you do open schools, teachers will die (exposure to multiple outside contacts)."

What the other school districts in the county were planning did not have a huge impact on Dr. Lind's choice, although he did not want to be the only district out on a limb (the only one to open, or the only one *not* to). Lake County superintendents met twice weekly, but there didn't appear to be any forthcoming decisions (it seemed like they were all waiting for the others to make the first move).

I know Dr. Lind was determined to get the students in at some point. It would be an understatement to say he prioritized in-person learning. Born and raised in Minnesota, he was famously known to be the lone holdout for snow days.

Although it would be complicated, he felt getting back in person was doable. He held multiple Zoom meetings throughout the summer to discuss the possibility and sent out surveys to get feedback from parents and staff.

As he explained to me later, the biggest hurdle was meeting the ever-changing CDC guidelines; as soon as one goal was met and he thought we were good to go, the goalpost would move. A huge roadblock involved N95 face masks, which were advised for all nurses, custodians, and any staff with compromised health. The problem was that there were no N95 masks available. You couldn't get them anywhere. And when the state finally sent a batch, the masks were defective.

The parents in our district overwhelmingly wanted their kids back in class (I got that!). *"But at what price?"* was all I could think about. It seemed to be a no-win situation, and the decision was taking forever.

Meanwhile, teachers were out on the ledge, but, incredibly, none quit, retired early, or took a Leave of Absence. My paraprofessional was among those support staff who retired; she had health issues and also realized that what she was being paid was certainly not worth the risk.

Finally, by the end of July, a decision was announced: we would open fully remote, with a gradual phase-in plan to commence the week after Labor Day. Parents could decide whether their children would be in person or remote, which meant some teachers may have to instruct both at the same time (blended). Special Education students, Early Childhood students, and kindergarteners would come back first (since these groups were the most negatively impacted by being remote), followed by grades one and two the next week. Third, fourth, and fifth graders would come in a week after that. Returns were staggered because the school district didn't want all the students converging in the building at once and wanted to get smaller groups of students used to the safety protocols before bringing in additional bodies.

New guidelines from the state helped fill in the rest of the details: instruction would be divided into four hours of "synchronous" (yes, another new buzzword, meaning live) learning in the morning and Specials classes (Art, Music, Gym) "asynchronous" (on demand) and done from home in the afternoons. Afternoons for non-Specials teachers would include prep and planning with teams, as well as meeting virtually with any students who were struggling and providing them another layer of support (since interventionists were now homeroom teachers).

I felt a little better, now that we had a plan.

I could, and would, suck it up. I didn't have a choice. But the thought of four hours of live teaching through Zoom was daunting.

7

TRANSITION #1: BEYOND WEIRD
AUGUST 2020: PART 1

A ugust = Sunday, often filled with dread, like when you know the weekend is almost over and thoughts turn to your busy workweek ahead.

The world seemed to blow up for us that month. Black Lives Matter protests had been increasing nation-wide since May. The death of African American George Floyd at the hand of a white Minnesota police officer had ignited not only national, but global, outrage.

Now the situation had hit way close to home. In nearby Kenosha, Wisconsin, another shooting of a Black man by a white police officer set off a protest that quickly got out of hand, with several people fatally shot and much of downtown Kenosha destroyed in the ensuing riot. The National Guard was brought in, mere miles from our home. Many of our favorite places in Kenosha had been looted and/or burned. It made national headlines.

It was too much to bear; what was happening? As if a pandemic alone wasn't enough to make us feel anxious, hopeless, and defeated.

It was beyond weird to go through traditional August preparations at school in this new realm. Since Kindergarten Screening is an integral part of organizing our classes, we had to formulate a plan for it in this time of COVID-19.

Screening involves giving each child a twenty-minute assessment, checking pre-reading skills (letter names, letter sounds, and sight words), number sense (counting and cardinality), and small motor skills (printing and cutting with a scissors). The screening results helped us section the incoming kindergartners into each class, with an equal number of "high," "average," and "low" scoring students going to each teacher.

The kindergarten team prepared to screen the incoming kindergartners through glass partitions, teacher and child masked (do you know how hard it is to discriminate letter sounds coming out of a kid in a mask?), disinfecting the area and materials after each appointment. Some parents were too nervous to even allow that, so their children were given virtual screenings. (One of the younger and less technology-challenged teachers took that on). We screened and sectioned around ninety kids.

Our class sizes were to be reduced significantly (fifteen to sixteen students each) to allow for six-foot distancing once the students began attending in person, so another teacher was added to our team (a teacher from the disbanded intervention team, one who usually taught remedial students). She would take most of the fully remote learners, those students whose parents wanted them e-learning the entire year. Because remote was so new, her class was purposefully made the smallest (twelve students).

Most kindergarten teachers would also have at least two remote students joining the class every day (making each class a "blended" learning environment). I somehow dodged that bullet and was assigned no remote students, but I suspected it would only be a matter of time. There were bound to be quarantining students at some point.

Welcome to School Night for kindergarten parents, traditionally held the night before the first day of class, was switched from in person to virtual for the year. Our team put together a slideshow covering all the important points of kindergarten (including new rules for online learning). All of us would use the slideshow, but we would each host our own meeting, introducing ourselves to our students' parents and trying our best to make our meetings somewhat personal.

That Zoom meeting was a disaster for me. What those parents must have thought! Even though I practiced and did a couple of run-throughs, my technological inexperience and nervousness made me extremely flustered. It was unfortunate that there was not one administrator or technology staff member in the building that evening (a miscommunication, apparently).

I had parents trying to give me tips—"Click this, click that, you're on mute!"—as I lost the slideshow (I had just learned how to share my screen that morning) and eventually lost them all as well. When I got everyone back, I went purely on memory (forget the slideshow).

There I was, the veteran member of the kindergarten team, looking foolish. I wondered if the parents could see my burning cheeks through the screen.

In a normal year, my Welcome to School Night goes smoothly (I'd done it over twenty times—I was a pro!). I actually enjoyed laying out the school day/year for the parents. I had become quite adept at answering the many questions only parents of kindergartners can pose. But this year, I found myself answering, "I don't know," or "That is to be announced," or "We are still figuring that out."

This year, this very un-normal year, I fled the school building in tears after my "presentation." I exploded to my husband in anger and frustration. I felt like a failure, and we hadn't even had the first day of class yet.

To make the first two weeks of remote school successful, the team knew we had our work cut out for us. We wanted the kids to have as authentic a kindergarten experience as possible, and that meant lots of hands-on activities. We had scoured every Dollar Tree store in the county (and even those in neighboring counties) for items to make up a Learning Box of supplies for each student, designed to keep everything in one place. We assembled small plastic containers for letters and sight words, a larger one for general supplies like pencils, scissors, crayons, and glue. A whiteboard, dry erase marker, and eraser. There were even containers for a Math Kit (number line, ten frame, counting cubes) and a Fine Motor Kit (hole punch, tweezers, Play-Doh).

The idea was that, when in-person learning began (this was allegedly meant to happen two weeks into the school year), all each kid had to do was pick up their box and bring it in. They would use it in class as well as at home, since there could be no shared supplies. What we didn't realize was that kindergartners couldn't manage that box on their own, especially on the bus; therefore, a drop-off by parents would later have to be organized.

For that first supply pickup, included with the box and an iPad/charger for each child would be a Learning Bag with separate Ziplock bags inside for each day of the week. Those contained any worksheets and/or art supplies for daily projects. A new Learning Bag would be prepped for the following week, to be made available when the finished week's bag was dropped off. Once again, teachers had problem-solved together. We had come up with a workable way to do kindergarten from home.

But what most people (including other teachers and administrators) don't realize or take into account is the unbelievable amount of front load preparation that is involved with kindergarten. Every year we have to be fully prepped before any other grade (while other grades have their Open House in September to cover curriculum and so forth, we do our presentation *before* school begins). And this year especially, we were absolutely frantic and frayed as we prepared the Learning Boxes.

There was so much to get ready! Writing names on workbooks, putting name labels on *everything*. Laminating a set of letters for each student (uppercase and lowercase) and then cutting them all out. Laminating nametags. (I have the best girlfriends in the whole world —I had them over for a Cutting Party + Wine + Pizza and we got it done!) Assembling the various kits for each and every student. Prepping the Learning Bags for the first week of school.

I wasn't the only one without an assistant—as luck would have it, all the kindergarten teachers, with the exception of one, had lost their assistants due to unrelated COVID-19 circumstances (one left to attend grad school, one was embarking on student teaching, one got a bona fide teaching job in another district). No one was applying for these assistant positions—what a surprise! The one assistant who remained was trying to the best of her ability to help us all.

Our kindergarten team was falling to pieces.

So it was no shock that, on the day of Supply Pickup, the team was in tatters. There were required Zoom meetings to attend that day as part of our beginning of the year in-service. We were drowning; without enough assistants to help, we desperately needed the prep time! Why in God's name should we have to listen to someone from the ROE (Regional Office of Education) rattling on about Math standards?? They were completely irrelevant to us that day.

During the afternoon session with the ROE, I spoke up. "I'm sorry, but I have parents showing up at 4:00

and I am not ready. We have teachers in tears down here. Thanks for your presentation, but I have to leave." One by one, my team followed.

Not long after, our superintendent, principal, and assistant principal came down to the kindergarten hallway. "What can we do?" It was a small gesture that went a really long way.

On that blazing hot August day (no shade to speak of in that parking lot), what had always been Supply *Drop-Off*/ Meet the Teacher became Supply *Pickup*/ Meet the Teacher. The parents drove through the school's back lot and were each directed to their child's teacher. I would find each child's box on my table and deliver it to the vehicle. If my student was in the car (most were), I did a meet-and-greet right there on the curb (feigning excitement—what can I say? I was sweating bullets and my feet were killing me. A complete blubbering breakdown hovered.)

"Hi [insert name]!"

"It's so nice to see you!"

"Don't you look pretty *(or handsome)* today!"

"I'm so excited to have you in my class!"

"Can't wait to see you on Zoom!"

At least I got a glimpse of the students before meeting them on the screen.

8

READY OR NOT

AUGUST 2020: PART 2

First Day of School 2020 looked like nothing I could have ever conjured up. I hardly slept the night before. That morning at 8:00, I couldn't seem to connect with my class via the link I had sent. What the @#$%?! I was sitting in a meeting by myself—where was everyone? Our Tech staff was off putting out other fires, so the principal came to my classroom, trying to help me. It was humiliating. I found out other teachers were having issues too. Something about Zoom being down? Did that happen? I don't know or remember. The principal reassured me it wasn't my fault (I think he was trying to prevent me from fleeing). All I know is, I got everyone into the same meeting. It might have been thirty minutes past the start time, but in we were, and off we went.

During those initial two weeks of remote teaching, I learned a lot, such as, *I am an actress*. I could win an award every day. No matter what my mood, when those doorbells rang and I clicked "Admit All," I had to *turn it on* and *turn it up*.

Also, kindergartners cannot sit still while attending class for four straight hours (honestly, who can??). They need movement breaks—and screen breaks. During our fifteen-minute screen breaks, I would tell the kids to go potty, get a snack, jump on the trampoline, ride their bikes. While they did, I would take a bathroom break, grab some more coffee, eat a banana... and talk to myself. I would hide my video and put up a return time on my Zoom whiteboard.

I remain ever thankful to the mom who messaged me during one break: "Mrs. P, you are not muted." Good lord, how embarrassing! I hope I didn't swear (but it's entirely possible). I never forgot to mute during breaks after that.

Another revelation was that what was so meticulously laid out in the daily lesson plan wasn't all going to get done. Most teachers over-plan; better to have too much planned than not enough. That was especially relevant this year.

So much of our time at the beginning of this year

was spent on teaching remote-learning etiquette, very similar to the rules and expectations we work on during the first few weeks when physically in school. A colleague shared some clever signs: "MUTE," "UNMUTE," "CAMERA ON." Over time, I was getting better at navigating Zoom. I had perfected screen-sharing, at least.

Now, if only that error message ("YOUR INTERNET CONNECTION IS UNSTABLE") could just stop popping up. I didn't know what to do with that!

"Sit up straight, boys and girls, faces in the screen."

"Honey, can you stop spinning in your chair? You're making Mrs. P dizzy."

"Can you come down from your bunk bed (or out of your blanket fort) and stay in your learning space?"

"Sweetie, keep your water bottle away from your device."

"Please don't unmute unless I ask you to." (*Boy, they figured that out quickly!*)

Other teachers on my team shared similar anecdotes. Yes, we all occasionally called kids by the wrong names. In my case, I often made the grave error of calling students by a sibling's name (since I'd often previously had my students' siblings in kindergarten). They did *not* appreciate that!

One teacher had us in stitches—for one whole week, she had assumed one child was a boy, when actually *she* was a girl (the child had one of those names that could be either).

"Is there ever going to be a day when you don't make a mistake?" a very serious, by-the-book boy asked yet another kindergarten teacher.

"Probably not, buddy," she replied. "Probably not."

As any teacher will tell you, success in teaching and managing a classroom relies heavily on forming a relationship with the students, creating your class "family," so to speak. You want all of your students to have a stake in the group's success. That was proving to be a bit challenging through a computer screen.

I tried to begin each day with an emotional temperature check: "How are you feeling today? Answer on your whiteboard with a happy or sad face and hold it up." I answered too. That would often lead to some meaningful discussion, although honestly, the students all seemed really happy and excited. This was how school was for them; they didn't know it any other way. In hindsight (which is always the best), these temperature checks would've been way more appropriate to do with the previous year's class, given the fact that their whole world had been upended overnight.

I wanted us to get to know each other, so next I would pose a Question of the Day. I would answer first and then let the students share, one at a time, if they wanted to.

"What did you have for breakfast?"

"What makes you happy/sad?"

"Do you have brothers and sisters?" (Those only children tend to stand out right away.)

"What is your favorite food?"

"What was the best thing you did over the summer?"

"What is your favorite thing to play?"

I taught the students our kindergarten songs and sang my silly heart out every day. It was a one-woman show. I love to sing but am not particularly good at it; thankfully, kindergartners don't recognize "off-key" when they hear it.

Most of my students needed firm adult support for learning activities. Moms and/or dads were handing them their supplies, cutting things out for them, and sometimes even managing the glue sticks (much to my dismay). Some were even feeding their kids during lessons, shoving bits of French toast at them or spooning cereal into their mouths as if they were baby birds while I babbled on and on. So much for the recommendation on Welcome to School Night: "Please don't allow your child to eat during Zoom lessons." (Perhaps I had neglected to mention that, given the frenzied state I was in that evening?)

I was blessed to have a paraprofessional assigned to two Special Ed students who mainstreamed into my class, and she helped out with *all* the kids. Sally was my "Co-Host with the Most" every day. Not only did she manage students coming in late (or leaving early), she was quite adept at muting those who loved to hear themselves talk. Sally always kept me smiling with the signs she made to hold up at just the right times during Zoom: "MARVELOUS MONDAY!" "TACO TUESDAY!" "FRIDAY! MRS. P'S FAVORITE DAY! YAY!"

Learning Bags were ready for pickup in the vestibule of the building every week from Thursday between 3:00 and 7:00 p.m. and Friday at 7:00 p.m. Parents would drop off the previous week's bags and pick up the ones for the upcoming week. Bags were continually recycled. Our system was good, but certainly not flawless.

Sometimes, the bags never came back. Sometimes, the bags were not picked up in time for Monday class. Occasionally, parents picked up the wrong bag—James' dad came to get his and accidentally took Jamie's bag. Not a big deal—all the bags were the same—except that Jamie's mom was freaking out because her bag "wasn't there."

One time, incredibly, a parent from one class took the entire box of Learning Bags (as in, *every single one*) so *nobody* in that class had their materials come Monday morning). I have yet to figure *that* one out. *Learn to adapt.*

While many teachers taught from home, I chose to teach from my classroom. We were lucky to have that option; I know teachers in many other districts were not allowed a choice in the matter.

There's just so much "stuff" involved with kindergarten! To do the best job possible, I felt that I needed to have easy access to said "stuff"— like my calendar pocket chart, number chart, easel and whiteboard, and magnet letters and numbers, not to mention all of my books. I was not about to haul it all home at this point! Plus, as came to light the previous spring, I needed a clear distinction between work and home for my mental well-being. Teaching from school kept me in a steady, familiar routine.

As I have said, teachers are champions at adapting and problem-solving. Did I also mention sharing? If you know where to look, you can find anything and everything to support your teaching. And that summer, amazing ideas related to e-learning were popping up like crazy. There were entire websites dedicated to just that.

Our team found a very simple idea online for how to turn your iPad into a document camera. Connect your iPad to your laptop, place your iPad upside down on a locker shelf, put the worksheet under the shelf, turn the iPad camera on, and share your screen. *Bam!* Show the work to the class up close, step by step. Brilliant.

So I made a teaching space in one corner of my classroom and positioned myself at the table, my computer on a lime-green plastic lap desk (for optimum height). I had also made my own Learning Box with the exact same supplies as the students had in theirs. "Take out your Wednesday bag; it looks like this, with a yellow sticker."

Everything I needed was right within my reach. When I needed to move the laptop, I put it on top of a cart and rolled it around. When I needed to show the class a close-up of something on the board, the "Spotlight" feature came in handy. Teaching, COVID-style.

Often, I would turn my camera around and show the children the classroom. "These are your tables where you will sit every day. There's room for your Learning Box in your very own personal space! And here are your cubbies, where you will put your backpack. Look, we even have our own bathroom. Aren't we lucky? I can't wait to see you here at school!"

Just when I was getting the hang of it—and blessedly getting the class into a routine—it was time to prepare for the students coming into the school building. I had very mixed feelings. I knew it was best to have the kids in class, but I fretted about the logistics of it all. Could we make it work?

The 2020–2021 MES Kindergarten Team (8/2020)

The Best Friends in the World! Laminating Party
(8/2020)

Kindergarten Learning Bin and Book Box (9/2020)

Kindergarten Artwork in the Hallway Once Again
(9/2020)

Hands-On Play in the Classroom (10/2020)

Happy and Busy During Free Time (10/2020)

Reminder to Laugh Every Day! (11/2020)

I've Got This (11/2020)

100th Day, Celebrated in Person! (2/2021)

Zooming in a Quarantined Cutie (2/2021)

Dose #2, Done! (3/2021)

Reading Group, COVID-Style (3/2021)

Co-Host with the Most, Sally (4/2021)

Butterfly Release Day (5/2021)

TRANSITION #2: WELCOME TO SCHOOL —FOR REAL!

SEPTEMBER/OCTOBER 2020

Getting the students to and from school was going to be challenging, but we are a small district (two schools) with our own fleet of school buses. It was pretty impressive, what was worked out; "learn to adapt" not only applied to teachers, but to everyone dedicated to our kids.

Children were assigned seats (every other one, siblings together), masked at all times. Drivers (also dutifully masked) would do the first run for K–2, then head out to pick up students in grades three through five. For that reason, we were put on a staggered start. After taking care of the elementary schoolers, the buses would then do the middle school runs. Some parents were not comfortable with the arrangement, so they drove their kids to school (which is the case in a normal year too, although not nearly as common as it was in this COVID year).

Students' temperatures were taken at all school entrances prior to coming into the building. If anyone had a fever, they were immediately sent home.

Mustang floor decals ("Protect the Herd") and stickers were placed on all the hallway floors, marking six-foot distancing for the lines of students entering in the morning and exiting at noon. We were technically not supposed to leave our classrooms during those four straight hours of learning.

Thankfully, our classroom had a bathroom. Other classes were put on a bathroom schedule. Can you imagine telling a kindergartner he has to hold it until a designated time? (I predicted many accidents. I know the pee-pee dance when I see it.)

Water fountains were covered with black garbage bags and what looked like crime scene tape: "OUT OF ORDER." Hand-sanitizing stations were placed strategically throughout the building. Of course, masks were to be worn at all times unless you were in your classroom alone with the door shut. Students were instructed to bring water bottles and extra masks in their backpacks. All teachers were given additional PPE to have on hand, just in case.

Our Health Office was moved to a larger space, with

partitions installed between cots. An additional nurse was added part-time. COVID-19 protocol was put into place: what to do if a student wets his pants, throws up, or exhibits any COVID symptoms. It was a lot to digest. It was a lot to remember. Mine had been the classroom closest to the Health Office for over twenty years (mere feet away); now it was located clear across the building. Kindergartners could never find the Health Office by themselves, and we had no assistants to take them there if the need arose. Sometimes I just had to call down there and have one of the nurses come to us. *Learn to adapt.*

I had to put a lot of things from my classroom into storage: the horseshoe table that also served as my desk, the play kitchen, the tool bench, the beanbag chairs. The building blocks and matchbox cars had to be packed up. The dolls (and all that came with them) and floor puzzles had to go. Luckily, one of our gymnasiums had been turned into a storage space, so I did not have to bring all the materials home.

I had to make sure students would be six feet apart while sitting at their tables, so tables that used to hold four or five students were now just for two. Extra tables were brought in, and a yellow masking-tape line was placed across the middle to mark each student's learning space. Tables were arranged diagonally in the room and, with the help of a yardstick, were placed so that the kids on either end would also be six feet apart. Red stickers were placed under the table legs to designate the distance and help keep the tables from shifting.

Teachers were given a sound field and a microphone to wear if we wished, which made us easier to hear and understand during instruction. We found out quickly how difficult it is to enunciate while masked. One of my favorite things is to read aloud to my students, but wearing a mask really put a damper on character voices and expression!

The Apple TV would prove to be infinitely helpful for projecting my laptop screen for morning announcements, lessons, and YouTube movement breaks. I had moved up in the world and had ditched the locker shelf set-up. Through the kindness of a colleague, I was now using a gooseneck device holder clamped to my counter —I didn't have a desk anymore, as my table was in storage—for sharing my iPad screen.

Masking up when running errands is one thing; masking up for five to six straight hours is another. Surprisingly, the students did really great with it (better than me). I struggled; I felt like I was suffocating. I would often have to change masks midway through the day, as mine would be soaking wet from my non-stop talking. I developed a rash around my mouth and was absolutely parched all day long.

Anyway, a masked world most likely seemed the norm to our kindergartners, as young as they were. It was also apparent that parents had heeded our advice and had gotten their children used to wearing masks for several hours at a time while at home to prepare for being in the classroom. Their masks were so cute— animal faces, superheroes, polka dots, emojis. (Somebody, somewhere, was making a killing off this pandemic, no pun intended.) We were allowed to give the students a mask break for ten to fifteen minutes during snack time, but getting them to stay seated while unmasked was a challenge.

"Raise your hand if you like Goldfish!" *(They loved to play teacher.)*

"I have a bagel. It has cream cheese! Who likes cream cheese?"

"Try and guess what I have!"

"My mom made me a muffin!"

"What do you have?"

"I have Pringles too!"

All this would be said while moving closer and closer to each other. I felt like the classic Bad Cop, and I couldn't take my eyes off the students for one minute.

"You there! Back away. Stay in your own space!"

The next thing I knew they could be sharing their food, which is a no-no even in a normal year.

I also let the students take off the masks when heading outside for walks to break up the morning (the playground was off-limits, cordoned off with the previously mentioned crime-scene-type tape). Thankfully, it was a lovely early fall, with copious amounts of sunshine. Sometimes I turned these walks into an "I Spy" game:

"I spy, with my little eye... something red."

"A van!"

"A leaf!"

Had you driven by our school in September or October 2020, you may have seen a line of small children "zombie walking" (arms outstretched in front of them) around the grounds. Sometimes, making our walks into a game was the only way to help the Littles maintain their distance.

Distancing was, by far, the hardest concept for the kindergartners to grasp. By nature, children that age get into each other's space when talking, eating, and playing. (Have you ever watched them play soccer? They *all* huddle around the ball and move down the field in one giant clump.)

Play is vital in early childhood, and in a normal year it is a very natural way for the kids to practice their social skills. But unfortunately, there was little to no playing going on that fall. So, with some brainstorming, the team came up with a viable option. I borrowed a storage cart with drawers from a colleague and filled the drawers with hands-on materials like Play-Doh and tools, wooden puzzles, LEGOs, stencils, craft stems and pony beads, pattern blocks, silly scissors and hole punches, magnetic tiles, and geoboards. When the kids finished their work early, they could each select a drawer and bring it to their learning space.

The introduction of the drawers was an immediate hit! The activities kept the kids happily occupied during their downtime. In keeping with protocol, students had to sanitize their hands prior to taking drawers, keep their drawers for the whole day (stashing them under their table during work time), and sanitize again after putting their drawers back in the cart.

I planned to change up the materials every few weeks, to keep the activities fresh for the students. This solution was far from perfect, since the kids weren't playing *with* each other. But at least they were having some social interaction, because of course they chatted the whole time. And of course I let them.

"Look at what I built!"

"Your (Play-Doh) cookies are ready!"

"Do you like the bracelet that I made? I'm going to give it to my mom!"

In addition to the lack of toys, another thing that was bothering me was the absence of books in the classroom —alphabet books, picture books, early readers, storybooks, fiction and nonfiction to go with every one of our themes. Oh, they were there, but sorted and packed into bins out of the kids' reach since they could not be shared. My shelves stood empty. Normally, kindergartners could sit on the carpet or in a beanbag chair and "read" books together during downtime. Clearly that wasn't going to happen this year.

Getting books into little hands is so important, even for children who are not reading any words yet! Turning pages, looking at pictures, and making up accompanying words goes a long way toward future reading success.

Yet again, teacher innovation to the rescue. I made up a book box for each student to keep in their learning space. I filled the boxes with twelve to fifteen books each, encompassing our fall themes (apples, pumpkins, Halloween), math (counting and patterns), science (life cycles of apples and pumpkins, seasons), and some good old favorites like Pete the Cat, Biscuit, and Dr. Seuss.

The children kept the collection for one week; on Fridays, they lined the boxes up on the counter. I let them sit over the weekend and then rotated them all on

Monday. Whenever the students started a new week, they would all have a new collection waiting for them.

The students really enjoyed their book collections; I loved it when they would find a certain book and excitedly exclaim, "Look! I've got this one! You read this to us!" or "I have this at my house!" Looking at their books became the perfect activity for the start of the day, as we waited for everyone to arrive and I went through my duties of submitting attendance and checking homework folders.

I had the dubious "honor" of having the student with the first known case of COVID-19 in the elementary building. I should have known there was bad news when I entered through the front doors on a Tuesday morning in late September to find the superintendent *and* the principal waiting right inside. Clearly, they were waiting for me.

(I was late a lot; Last-Minute Lucy, that's me. But that day, I was right on time.)

"Good morning Mrs. P!" *(Way too chipper...)*

"Good morning, what's going on?" *(Hackles up, what now?)*

As they filled me in, I actually felt faint. I remember

placing my hand on the wall to steady myself. This was it. I had most certainly been exposed. Well, that hadn't taken long.

No one knew where the child had contracted COVID. No one in the home had it; both parents worked from home, and the family never went anywhere. But the county health department would keep up contact tracing efforts.

With COVID-19 protocol and CDC guidelines continually evolving (I couldn't keep up with them), it was uncertain what would happen next. Had the child been in the classroom the previous day, we would have had to move everyone to an alternate space and the classroom would have to be deep-cleaned, but he had been out since the previous Friday. Thus, tables, chairs, and counters should not, in theory, contain traces of COVID-19.

By now it had been determined that the virus didn't live long on non-porous surfaces. Sanitizing was still important, but masking and distancing were paramount. Also, at that time, young children were thought to be "Super-Spreaders." They could be infected but remain asymptomatic.

The affected student would have to isolate for four-teen days, and it was determined that the two children sitting nearest him would have to quarantine too. This was confusing (they were so carefully spaced apart)! The way it was explained to me was that, because they were unmasked for a fifteen-minute period (for Snack) and they were no doubt talking (shouting) to each other, respiratory droplets may have been exchanged, so isolation was indicated for all three children.

I asked, "What about the teacher??"

I always walked around the room when teaching, sometimes going hand-over-hand to correct a pencil grip or scissor grasp. I couldn't remember if I had had contact with that particular child. Most likely! Probably!

Unbelievably, I did not have to isolate *or* take a COVID-19 test, but I could if I wished. Of course I was going to get tested! I was advised to wait at least five days. During those days, I was teaching twelve in class and three online... and trying not to panic. Good times. *Learn to adapt.*

During those five days, I had no symptoms whatsoever. At home, my husband chased me around, pointing a thermometer at my forehead every couple of hours. Each morning, the first words out of his mouth were, "How do you feel?" *Good God, cross as usual.* (I am *not* a morning person). *Stop talking!*

I was able to get a drive-through test at a site in a nearby community. After waiting almost two hours in a line that snaked out of the parking lot and down the street, I was handed a Q-tip and given instructions. There was about a forty-eight-hour turnaround from swab to results. It was negative. Thank you, Jesus!

Twice that fall, I would end up having to relocate my class to the empty Music room and have my classroom deep-cleaned after sending students home with COVID-19 symptoms. Neither of those incidents developed into anything, thank goodness.

There were sporadic cases here and there in other grade levels, but very few students and only some family members of students were impacted. Most of the staff got used to having kids Zooming in from home due to quarantining.

It was a challenging time for everyone; "learn to adapt" was taking on a whole new meaning. I felt bad for the students on the screen because I knew I would never be able to give them enough of my attention—not while managing an in-person kindergarten classroom and all that that involves (spilled water bottles, broken pencils, missing glue caps, tying shoes, replacing the paper towel roll in the bathroom)—especially without an assistant. Sally was great at jumping in when she could, but her two charges kept her busy.

The kids in class would let me know: "So-and-so is raising her hand," or, "So-and-so needs you, Mrs. P!"

Sometimes I would hear a child or a parent calling

out, "Mrs. P? Excuse me, Mrs. P? What should we be doing now?" from my computer across the room. It was easy to forget about the virtual learners.

Late in October, there was a rash of COVID-positives at our building. A group of staff members had gone out on a Friday after school to a restaurant/bar in Wisconsin (we are four miles from the border).

COVID guidelines were a whole different story up there—it was "wide open," so to speak. Establishments in Wisconsin were up and running like nothing was amiss, business as usual. Some places did not even require masks at that time. (Different state, different mandates. It all seemed so crazy to me.) I understood the appeal; we were all longing to get out and socialize normally. I am certainly not judging. However, several of the staff members who had gone out became ill, a few very seriously, and one was even hospitalized. Seventeen staff would end up in quarantine. Luckily, all were support staff, so securing substitutes for classrooms was not an issue. Subs were somehow worked out for the affected bus drivers. It was quite scary though. It felt like the virus was closing in.

I know that our superintendent was feeling frustrated because some families were not adhering to guidelines either; there were rumors circulating of neighborhood gatherings and kids' birthday parties taking place in our school community every weekend.

People (me included) were tired of isolating. We were nine months into this pandemic, and everyone was sick of it.

The positivity rate continued to climb in our area, just as it did nationally. The sheer number of cases—and deaths—was soaring. Illinois reverted to our previous lockdown status. Therefore, the decision was made to go back to remote learning beginning November 2nd. I think Dr. Lind was hopeful we could come back after a couple of weeks, but reality spoke otherwise. We would be dealing with the upcoming Thanksgiving break (more gatherings, travel, possible exposure) and then winter break (same). Dr. Lind, as well as the majority of staff, knew in our hearts we would be out for a good while.

Ultimately, we would return to learning January 4, but we would remain remote until mid-January 2021, allowing students a built-in two-week quarantine after the holidays.

One bright spot that month, though: news of two prospective COVID-19 vaccines rolling out soon.

10

TRANSITION #3: BACK TO REMOTE
NOVEMBER/DECEMBER 2020

Those eight weeks we had had the kids in school, while stressful, were glorious. They were the closest thing to normal we could've hoped for. Not only did the time in person allow us teachers to get a real handle on what our students could/could not do, it gave us time to build relationships with them. I was blessed to have fifteen very sweet, very easy kids. I felt like I wasn't heading into this second remote stretch *so* blind.

A contentious presidential election wasn't helping matters as we headed back to remote learning though. Pile on the stress! There was so much at stake! I could not believe what was unfolding before our eyes on the nightly news after Election Day: the election results were being contested even before they were fully counted, and rumors swirled that sitting President Trump might not concede if the election was not declared in his favor. I felt we desperately needed new, more empathetic leadership to get us to the other side of this pandemic. In my lifetime, I had never seen a losing presidential candidate refuse to concede. This needed to be settled, the sooner the better, for everyone's sanity. We teachers hid our anxiety well, waiting to tune into the latest updates after class. My students, of course, had no clue what was going on beyond their own little worlds—as it should be.

I was back in my little corner of the classroom, getting more comfortable with virtual teaching as the weeks passed, but not liking it any better. We emailed progress reports to parents and conducted conferences online (unthinkable to me not so long ago).

I mastered managing breakout rooms on Zoom during instruction, a feat I was extremely proud of. Since there had been no school pictures, everyone—staff and students—was instructed to take a selfie for the yearbook and sent the link to do so. *Learn to adapt.*

Despite occasional mishaps, technology was a better friend to me this time around. Less and less often was I hearing, "We can't see the screenshare!" or, "Mrs. P, you're glitchy!" or my favorite, "You're frozen-ing!"

The students were not relying *so* much on their

parents to do their tasks, although it was hard to tell how much they were really getting done independently or even finishing completely. Moms and dads had left their children's sides but usually remained nearby, within earshot.

Of course, staff meetings of all kinds continued, always virtually. I will give the administrators an "A" for effort for their thoughtful breakout room questions, games, and STRONG (Staff Together Reaching Out to Nurture and Grow) meetings twice a week.

But honestly, who feels like staying late on a Friday afternoon to play trivia on Zoom after an exhausting week of teaching? I couldn't tell you anything about STRONG meetings because I never attended one. According to our principal, Ben Walshire, the administrators' goal was to identify and help any staff members who might be struggling during this time. "They needed outlets and avenues to connect," he explained. That may be good for some, but meeting online with random people is not my thing.

We didn't want to fill out an online form every week letting an admin know how we were feeling. How about coming down in person and checking? Some of us felt that was not too much to ask.

It was a bit disconcerting, at least to us on the kindergarten team, that there were always multiple to-do lists and "Mark These Dates" and "Talk With Your Team About (blah-blah)"s. This year, of all years, maybe we could take some stuff off our plates?

There is no doubt there is business that needs to be attended to in the process of running a school, but "there's a way, and there's a way." Mr. Walshire later shared that he had been totally open to taking items off the to-do list and that he had been hesitant to introduce any new initiatives at that time. Apparently, we should have spoken up.

Why were we having professional development days to meet with someone from the ROE (Regional Office of Education) to dissect our assessment tools (formative or summative—honestly, at that moment, who cared?)? How was discussing Spring Assessment schedules helping me in the moment? Really, you want us to update supply lists for school year 2021–2022?

And don't even get me started on the fact that we were even considering doing standardized testing this year. Thank goodness kindergartners did not have to take the various mandated state tests; however, we would still be administering MAP, Measures of Academic Progress.

The primary focus this school year was supposed to be Social/Emotional Health for students *and* teachers.

Why were we talking about closing achievement gaps this year of all years?

Isolated in our individual classrooms during these meetings, my fellow team members and I would often text amongst ourselves.

"I'm falling asleep." *[sleeping face emoji]*

"What is he talking about?" *[eyeroll emoji]*

"Is it too early for wine?" *[wine emoji]*

"Or a drink?" *[martini glass emoji]*

"Make it stoppppp!" *[anguished face emoji]*

"So much for self-care." *[weeping face emoji]*

I'm sorry, but feelings are feelings. We were on Complete Overload and just trying to make it through Today. Next Year was unthinkable, let alone Tomorrow!

There was little differentiation in instruction happening at this time. I had completed the first trimester assessments right before the kids went back to remote learning, so I had a good handle on where they all were.

It was simply very challenging to meet with small groups via Zoom. Kinders cannot go into a breakout room and work independently while the teacher meets with a group; they need adult supervision. Luckily, Sally helped me out with that when we could manage it.

Meanwhile…

"I don't have that paper. Moooommmy! I need help!" (*Sweetie, yes you do. Look again.*)

"My Thursday bag is empty." (*What?! I'm pretty sure we didn't give you an empty bag.*)

"I can't find my markers. Can I use a dry erase one?" (*Oh lord. Not on paper, hon.*)

"I lost my glue stick, so I am using this runny stuff. And it has glitter in it!" (*Awesome.*)

The pandemic raged on. It was during this stretch that the kindergartners became quite tech "sassy." More and more were turning off their cameras (a strategy which, I cannot lie, sometimes comes in handy during staff Zooms) and inexplicably leaving meetings and coming back in ("I got kicked out.").

A student showed up with a virtual background on her Zoom one morning. Her mom explained, "We have to be in the basement today because we have repairmen upstairs. And our basement is a mess!" She had changed the background to a luscious rainforest scene.

"Ooooh! How did you do that?" All the kids wanted to know.

So of course I was obligated to teach myself virtual backgrounds (with Sally's help) so I could show the kids how. The students played around with their back-grounds for a day or so (some were really into it; some could've cared less) until I had to put the kibosh on that. Way too distracting.

"You know we can all see you, right?" I said to the kid standing up on a chair waggling his pajamaed bottom at the camera. I also said it to the one gleefully digging in her nose. "Get a tissue, sweetie."

In December, it really struck me how isolating this type of teaching is. Basically, I was sitting in my classroom alone and talking to myself for four straight hours every day. I missed seeing coworkers and I missed my team (two had packed it up and were teaching from home). The camaraderie and basic human interaction were notably absent.

Those of us remaining in the K hallway could not even eat lunch together; we were instructed not to gather and to eat lunch in our classrooms with the doors closed. I looked forward to seeing the team on Mondays —the one day we met in person to do planning. We had our designated spots in each corner of the room, one in the middle, with the remote teacher Zooming in. We stayed masked at all times.

It was at one of these meetings that the superintendent popped in to share the vaccine rollout plan for Lake County educators. At last!! We were part of Frontline Essential Workers Group B, following those in Group A (first responders and health care workers). The details would probably change ten times, but for now the plan was to begin inoculations in late January at two county high school pods. We were encouraged to register online with the county health department. Once we were in the system and vaccine doses began arriving, an appointment could be scheduled at one of the designated locations. We wouldn't have a choice as to which vaccine we received (Pfizer or Moderna); we would get whichever one was available. It would be several weeks before the Johnson & Johnson vaccine would become available in our area. (That one was very appealing to some people —"one and done," no second shot needed, unlike the two doses required for Pfizer and Moderna.)

On Zoom, the students continued eating, spinning, and occasionally disappearing. With Christmas coming, keeping them focused was a daily challenge. It was downright exhausting. The parent craft/gift we tried to make with them virtually was lame and not at all up to our usual standards.

It was going to be a very different holiday season for all of us; it had been nearly a year since Joe and I had seen our extended family, and we would obviously not be getting together this year. The sole redeeming factor of Zoom and FaceTime (connecting in real time) was that they had at least allowed us to keep in touch with our siblings and friends these past ten months. I tried to muster up enthusiasm.

My Kinders did not seem fazed in the least by the shadow of the pandemic. Santa was coming, COVID or no COVID! Yay!!

With just one week to go until winter break, a kindergarten teacher tested positive for COVID-19, a first for our team. She was not experiencing symptoms, but was tested as a precaution because her son had contracted the virus.

Since she was one of us who had been teaching from school, her diagnosis was a little concerning. Although we passed each other in the hallway every day and often chatted and met weekly at our planning meeting, I felt we had been sensible and careful (always distanced, always masked).

She quarantined, teaching from home, and thankfully her symptoms were mild. None of us was required to get a COVID-19 test, but it was just another scary reminder about this virus: you could be walking around infected and not even know it.

I would end up having my second COVID test the very next week (as would Joe) because my son and his girlfriend, Anneliese, had turned up positive. We had recently spent time with them at the Christmas tree farm. Having someone in your personal bubble contract the virus is very troubling indeed!

We tested negative, but that Christmas Day was rather bleak, as Eddie and Anneliese were quarantining. Lizzie had moved out over the summer and was spending the day with her boyfriend and his family, so Joe and I ate the Christmas cappelletti alone.

Fortunately, the kids' symptoms were not acute, and both Eddie and Anneliese recovered without incident. We postponed our family Christmas celebration until New Year's Day. Everyone got gimmicky masks as stocking stuffers (Rolling Stones lips for Joe, a kitty face for Lizzie, and an elephant for Eddie). Our traditional fare (made weeks before) was pulled from the freezer and reheated, and the Christmas tree was practically dead by then. *Learn to adapt.*

11

TRANSITION #4: HAPPY NEW YEAR?

JANUARY 2021

We opened school for 2021 with remote learning, which would continue until after the Martin Luther King, Jr. holiday (mid-January). The plan was to phase in, just like the previous fall. After eight weeks of online school and three weeks of holiday breaks (Thanksgiving and Christmas), I think everyone was ready—especially parents.

For me, all the political unrest that was happening in our country proved to be a huge distraction from the task at hand. The U.S. Capitol was violently stormed by a mob of former President Donald Trump's supporters in an attempt to overturn his defeat—on the very day that Congress was assembled to count electoral votes to formalize Joe Biden's victory. What the @#$%?! 2021 was supposed to be better!! We were a mere six days in and the @#$% was already hitting the fan. I watched the news reports in absolute disbelief. I pushed all thoughts of impending doom from my mind and tried to stay focused on teaching about penguins—because learning must carry on.

With this phase of Return to Learn, staff members were required to self-certify that we were healthy online each day before entering the building: no COVID-19 symptoms to report. Parents were supposed to do the same for their children. It got a bit dicey: So yeah, I have a headache, just like pretty much every day of this crazy school year. Fatigue? Most certainly. Congestion? Allergies. Stomach upset? Always. COVID-19? Highly doubtful. Basically, we all turned into liars.

There was a lot of reteaching of procedures and expectations that needed to be done once we were back in in-person classes. It had been a long time since we were all together in the same room.

There was no mute button.

The students were at a lower level academically than is usual for January. Sight words weren't sticking. We were struggling with tasks like writing simple sentences. I was dismayed at the state of the students' handwriting. (It's so hard to teach letter formation through a screen!) None of this was surprising.

Also, independence and confidence were noticeably lacking; I'm going to go out on a limb and attribute that to learning from home as well. The students wanted us to walk them through *everything*. That, and tell them all the answers.

The "deer-in the headlights" look when I said, "You can spell that word yourself."

The blank faces when I said, "What do you think will happen next?"

The gaping mouths when I asked them to write *anything*.

"I don't like this" when they were requested to do something challenging. Or even "I don't want to (do this)." Seriously? "I don't want to"??

Self-help skills were noticeably lacking all around. There were string cheese wrappers and empty yogurt tubes abandoned on tables daily, crumbs and popcorn kernels ground into the carpet. Markers and glue sticks were left open to "dry" a slow death, while the floor was littered with their missing caps. It was a good thing the custodians liked me.

"Honey, do you have a glue stick?" *[Shrug.]*

"Where is your iPad?" *[Shrug]* "My mom didn't pack it."

"Your iPad is only on 10% battery power?" "Well, I told my daddy to charge it, but he didn't."

Boys and girls would sit idle and wait for me to come over and pack up their things for them at the end of the day.

"My stuff won't fit in my backpack."

"I can't zip *(or unzip)* my coat."

"I can't find my other glove!"

"Somebody took my other boot!"

The students' parents had been so wonderful at keeping them together and organized during remote learning. Now these kids had little to no idea how to do things for themselves. No blaming here—we were all doing the best we could. Our students were blessed to have parents who were involved.

Granted, in normal times some children are still needy at this point in the school year, but never so many as this. "Let's be problem-solvers" became our class mantra. It took a lot of patience and deep breaths—back to square one. Meet them where they are.

On the positive side, kindergarten was racking up the best attendance record ever. Chalk that up to mask-wearing when we were together, being apart from each other for weeks on end, and the simple fact that parents were ready for a break. I rarely had anyone absent.

On the negative side, the elementary building was having major water issues. The first week we were back in school, strange things were popping up; namely, black water in the toilets. Many a terrified kindergartner came running out of our bathroom with the news. "The water is all dirty! I didn't do it!"

Apparently, the blackness was due to sediment; there was a break in the pipeline from the well that supplied the west section of the elementary building, *our* section. The water supply was turned off while this was being investigated, which meant our students had to use the bathrooms in the east section of the building. Tricky indeed.

We had "runners" who would take our kids to the bathrooms as needed. Kinders need to go a lot! I was texting helpers constantly. It was a complete disruption to our day. I would have to stop instruction midstream for bathroom runs. Let's face it, when you ask a class of kindergartners, "Who has to go?" they *all* line up. It's an adventure! There was not a lot of learning going on.

These kids were such troopers. They had been through so many transitions this school year, and they rolled with the punches of the broken bathrooms —happily.

A new water line was run from the well and the water was turned back on, only for toilet use for the moment. If the kids used the water to wash their hands, they needed to sanitize too. (*Seriously?*)

Then, as if a busted underground pipe wasn't

enough, there was also a leak in the water tank that supplied the west side of the building. Thousands of gallons were being lost every day, so water was being brought in via tanker truck every few days to refill it. To help curb the loss from the tank, the water was turned off at night and turned on again in the morning; this pressure caused dirt and sediment to pop up and clog the flushing mechanism on the toilets. We could once again use our classroom toilet, but it would continuously flush... and flush... and flush, a roaring noise that would send students bursting out of the bathroom, wide-eyed. "It won't stop!!"

The custodian was called, and by banging on the pipes a certain way in a certain spot with a hammer, she could get the valve to close and the constant flushing to cease.

I, too, learned to use my trusty pink hammer to pound on the pipes as needed. Yay! The kids thought it was great. "Mrs. P, you solved the problem yourself!" Minimal learning happening, but there was lots of clapping and cheering.

The second week we were back in school, yet another K teacher tested positive for COVID-19. Interestingly enough, she and I had been complaining of the same annoying symptoms at our Monday planning meeting.

Both of us had spent much of that Sunday in bed with debilitating headaches and congestion. I was beside myself; I couldn't seem to taste my toothpaste or smell my hot lemon tea. Luckily, that was temporary; after I took a decongestant, those sensations came back.

By Monday, my fellow teacher and I felt well enough to come in to work (no fever). My colleague attributed her symptoms to her allergies and I swore mine were caused by a humdinger of a sinus infection.

On a weird hunch, my team member had a rapid test done that Monday afternoon. She was shocked when the result was positive. "Please forgive me for exposing you!" she typed on the K team group text.

This led me to get my own rapid COVID-19 test (my third) the next day. I went for my test in a mall parking lot; it was drive-through with no wait, and this time a nurse did the swab. While my previous tests had been free, this one cost a whopping $175 (submittable to insurance with a receipt).

I sat in my parked car and waited twenty minutes for the result. I needed to know *now*; I couldn't wait two days!

I thought for sure I was going to be positive since I had the same exact symptoms as my co-worker. I sat there planning what I would say to my principal. "So,

Ben. Are you sitting down?" But, surprise, my test came back negative.

When I messaged my doctor with the details and test result, along with a request for an antibiotic, she was skeptical. "I think your symptoms could be due to COVID-19," she said in an email. Apparently there were lots of false negatives with the rapid test. So I got another test (my fourth), this one a RT-PCR test (the "gold standard," which detects genetic material that is specific to the virus) at a local CVS. Two days later, that also came back negative. My doctor filled a prescription for an antibiotic—finally. She told me that she hadn't prescribed a Z-Pak in months. But, despite mask mandates, people like me were still getting sick with typical run-of-the mill crud that was unrelated to COVID-19.

January was cold and depressing and seemingly never-ending. But then there was a very thoughtful gesture by admin at our monthly staff meeting.

After everyone had logged into the Zoom meeting, we were asked to answer this question in the chat: "If you had an hour to do something for yourself right now, what would it be?" Many people answered "Sleep," or "Read a book," or "Cook my family a nice dinner."

I contemplated typing "Wine."

Then—surprise! The principal and assistant principal

released us all and told us to go do something to take care of ourselves. It was way too early for happy hour, so I went home and binged a few episodes of *Little Fires Everywhere* on Hulu. And... I may have had a glass of wine.

12

ALL-IN

FEBRUARY 2021

y February 8th, the phase-in was complete and
Millburn Elementary had all students from EC
(Early Childhood) through fifth grade back in
the building (minus those who had elected to be remote
for the year). We were only one week delayed due to the
water problems, which were now fixed.

We had been having a fairly mild winter up till that
point, but February brought record snowfall, storm after
storm. Temperatures plunged; it was subzero for one
whole week. It added insult to injury for adults (would it
ever end??), but the snow was a blessing for the kids, as
they were able to get outside—away from screens—and
play. I was heartened to hear their stories: sledding,
skiing, and snowman and snow fort building.

On the downside, there would apparently never be

another snow day. Remote learning had seen to that. Instead of, "Wake up, there's no school! Put on your snow gear and go out and play!" it was, "Wake up and log on!" What had been a glorious rite of passage in childhood was now a thing of the past, probably permanently. Why would the district add more days to the school calendar in June if they didn't have to? (Some people had a real problem with those added days. Me, not so much. Last day June 1st or June 3rd—who cares?)

My kindergartners would never get to experience an authentic snow day and the sheer joy of the last-minute cancellation of school. Teachers wouldn't, either. I used to pay close attention to the winter weather forecast, but not anymore. It made me kind of sad.

It was rather startling how many parents (school-wide, not just kindergarten) seemed to be clueless regarding the circumstances of having their children Zoom in to class for the day (or days). Now that we were back in person, information had been communicated to families (more than once!) that only if the student was quarantining due to COVID-related issues were they able to virtually join the class. But requests were made on a daily basis, in all grades, usually via email, often at 8:05 a.m. (school starts at 8:00).

"[insert any name here] will do school from home today due to the cold temperatures."

"We are in the Dells for a few days. The kids will Zoom."

"We are closing on a new house. [insert name here] will be virtual from our hotel for the week."

"We had a late night at a hockey tournament. Can my son Zoom in for today?"

Um, *no*. Your student will have to be marked absent, just like in a normal school year. Teachers were starting to feel a bit taken advantage of.

This had been a non-issue when we were in person the previous fall. I attribute that to the fact that, back *then*, parents were unbelievably happy to have their kids out of the house in school for at least part of the day.

And, more to the point, it wasn't snowing and below zero last October.

We had come to the time of year in which kindergarten students are ready to take all the skills they learned in the first trimester (letters and sounds, blending and segmenting, reading strategies) and put them into action. It was the time of year when we typically started meeting with reading groups.

At least I was able to meet with small groups now that we were back in person (such as it was). I would gather two to three students in my "office" (a little alcove in the front of the room) and do guided reading. The kids were thrilled to be getting little leveled books to take home and read. I was thrilled they were getting the much-needed practice.

"Your office is messy, Mrs. P!" *(No need to tell me that; I was aware.)*

"Are those pictures of your kids? They're old."

"Is your lunch in that fridge? What did you bring?"

"There's a spider on your ceiling." *(There goes the lesson.)*

It was comforting to know that some things never change.

But some things sadly stayed the same. Reminders to complete our required online GCN (Global Compliance Network) training? Sorry, the last thing on my mind was video training on such subjects as bloodborne pathogens, diabetes awareness, and ADHD (same as every year). New in this year of COVID-19 was a tutorial on handwashing *(I was an expert at this point.).*

Some colleagues received "the invitation" from Lake County Health Department during the first week of February, letting them know that they could make vaccination appointments. When you were summoned depended on when you had registered with the health department. The rollout was going slowly; Dr. Lind said we had to be patient. The snowstorms were certainly not helping—delivery of doses was delayed.

I was checking my email several times a day *(Had I*

clicked the wrong thing when registering?) and finally heard on February 10th that I could schedule my first dose. I made the appointment for the next day. Bring it!

On a frigid afternoon, I made my way into a local high school gymnasium, navigating the huge piles of snow and icy sidewalks. I showed up at the designated entrance right at my appointment time, appropriately distanced from the person in front of me.

I was impressed at how streamlined the process was. So organized! Twenty-five minutes, including the fifteen-minute wait time after inoculation, observed closely by paramedics in an auxiliary gym. My second dose would follow approximately twenty-eight days later. I had no side effects except a sore upper arm, similar to a flu shot. You do what you gotta do.

By the last week in February, the positivity rate in our region was under 4%, the lowest since July 2020. 65% of Millburn staff had received the first dose; 80% would be fully vaccinated by end of March at the conclusion of spring break.

Of course there were staff members who had no intention of getting vaccinated. Some didn't trust that the shot was safe. Others never got a flu shot, so they sure as heck weren't going to get this one. Some were quick to imply that getting vaccinated would most likely not protect against the new variants of COVID that were showing up. The one justification for opting out of the vaccine that bothered me the most: "I've already had COVID, so I'm good." Yeah, but what about everyone else? Herd immunity is a team effort! It was really difficult for me to understand that mindset, but I tried not to judge.

Personally, I felt getting the vaccine was the right thing to do, for the common good. It seemed to me to be the only way toward herd immunity and eventual eradication of the virus. I was more than willing to do my part.

But I was not totally naïve; I watched the national news every night and was aware of the new strains in the UK and Brazil and South Africa. Like all viruses, this one was mutating and changing at a rapid rate. The drug companies would no doubt have to change up the vaccine accordingly. I simply figured that, similar to being vaccinated against new strains of the flu, we would have to get an annual COVID-19 shot as well.

13

DÉJÀ VU
MARCH 2021

I n the kindergarten hallway, the team members once again found ourselves hanging green and gold shamrocks. We were all very quiet, each lost in the same thought: flashing back to March 2020, when we had *no* clue what was coming our way and had no idea that those shamrocks would not be taken down until the summer.

Had it really been one whole year since this all started? In many ways, it felt like a hundred years had passed. So much in our world had had to change, and everyone had learned to adapt in one—or many—ways. (Good grief, I'd let my hair go gray!)

Many are emerging from this year of COVID damaged to some extent: repurposed or lost jobs, family businesses that didn't make it. (Navigating the unemployment system is an exhausting feat in itself.) Some have lost loved ones to COVID-19; some are dealing with the "long haul" after-effects of COVID, like brain fog, exhaustion, and persistent anxiety. Many, many families have been separated from loved ones for over a year.

Everyone has emerged changed. Priorities have shifted (slowing life down and sticking close to home, while tedious at times, is refreshing in its simplicity). One thing I have taken away from it all: humans, especially kids, are a resilient lot.

As resilient as children can be, I remained very concerned for what the far-reaching ramifications would be from this time of COVID. These kindergartners had missed out on so many social learning experiences during the past year. They basically stayed home all the time—few if any had playdates. There was no going out to restaurants or stores; there were no excursions to museums or the aquarium or movie theaters. No opportunity to play with peers from other classes on the playground or to interact with classmates during lunch in the cafeteria. This is how our early childhood students learn how to navigate in the world: by observing and practicing expected behavior when out in public; by speaking to unfamiliar people, making eye contact and responding respectfully; by experiencing the give and take while playing with friends and figuring out how to appropriately handle not getting their way all the time.

The kindergarten teachers had noticed a sharp decline in the children's stamina for anything, especially that of the remote students. Feeling frustrated? You can't just run away from your screen, not in real life. We feared next year was going to be a difficult transition back to the classroom for these students.

On the personal side, it seemed unreal that it had been one year since I had hugged my brother or gone to a concert or out for Friday cocktails with coworkers. One of the things I missed the most (besides live music) was simply going out to a restaurant for dinner. I counted down the days and anxiously awaited the email that would tell me I could make an appointment for my second shot.

Exactly one week before my second dose was due, I got notification from the health department that I could schedule the appointment. But it was proving more difficult this time around; every time I logged in, there were no appointments available for times that suited me. (Yeah, I was being stubborn. I had long-awaited plans with girlfriends that I didn't want to postpone, cancel, or ruin with possible post-vax issues.) The site was updated with new appointments every day as additional doses were received, but I wasn't having much luck at either of the available pod locations. I knew I had at least a three-week window; the second shot didn't need to be administered *exactly* twenty-eight days after the first.

Finally I was able to snag a slot for March 17. Happy St Patrick's Day to me! I really didn't want a mid-week appointment, but took what I could get.

I was filled with much trepidation this time around. Having heard the stories from colleagues who had already received the second shot, I was nervous. Most had negative side effects, some more severe than others. Bottom line: I knew dealing with any bad side effects was better than contracting the virus. I was tough.

I am a fourteen-year breast cancer survivor and am no stranger to nasty side effects. I endured four rounds of chemo and thirty-three consecutive days of radiation and had emerged stronger for it. I am no wimp. I would be fine.

Not. Just three hours after my second dose, it hit me like a ton of bricks. Aches in my joints and long bones. Continuous, dull, debilitating pain. It felt like my skin was raw—*don't touch me!* No appetite to speak of. By the time I fell into bed, I had a fever. My husband said I moaned in my sleep all night long. It was unpleasantly reminiscent of the days I would receive a Neulasta injection following a chemo session. That shot stimulated white blood cell growth to stave off infection, and it made my long bones scream in distress. But this time, I had no prescription pain medication available to me.

The aftereffects of the vaccine lasted about thirty-six hours; the exhaustion lasted longer. I took March 18th off work and slept most of the day away. It was about five days before the lethargy finally faded and I felt back to my normal self.

I know this means the vaccine was doing its work. A small price to pay in the grand scheme of things.

EPILOGUE: MOVING FORWARD

A NOTE FROM APRIL 30, 2021

At this writing, with vaccine availability now opening up to everyone age sixteen and over, I feel hopeful. Although I don't think this pandemic is anywhere near over and I'm aware that *everyone* is tired of it all, we cannot afford to backslide by not adhering to CDC guidelines.

The head of the CDC is warning of a potential fourth wave, given the uptick in travel and the loosening (or absence) of restrictions in all states. Dr. Anthony Fauci, noted immunologist and director of the National Institute of Allergy and Infectious Disease, is imploring people to endure mask-wearing a while longer, especially when out in public. Those who have been fully vaccinated are now permitted to gather without masks.

Restaurants have opened, with limited capacity and

mask mandates in place. That is a hopeful sign! Some concerts and summer festivals are back on local schedules. 25% of the Illinois population has been fully vaccinated.

It is uncertain what the future holds, but I choose to remain strong and positive. We have all adjusted to new realities; we can never go back to the normal we knew before 2020. I'm not sure how one would even define "normal" these days.

Right now, we continue to teach in person; fingers crossed we will make it till summer break. Then this very stressful year of pandemic teaching will come to a close, and the biggest take-away will be this: *we survived!!* We accomplished what so many of us thought was downright impossible. Millburn District 24 proved that schools *can* safely open.

Our school nurses report that they have sent home upwards of four hundred students this school year with COVID-19 symptoms. Not one of those ended up with a positive COVID diagnosis, lending proof to the fact that, when proper protocol is followed, schools are not a source of virus spread. Most of our kids who quarantined did so due to positive cases in other family members or other close contacts outside of school.

The kindergarten team is preparing to give students the MAP test, a web-based assessment that is aligned to the Common Core standards, next month. It was a district decision to administer this test to all students K–5; the goal is to gage learning loss (where are the gaps?) during the past year. Oh, there will be gaps.

In kindergarten, we are growing butterflies in the classroom and are "waiting for wings." The radishes we planted from seed are flourishing on the classroom windowsill. The students' book collections have flipped several times over; they are currently enjoying fiction and non-fiction stories about weather, spring, insects, and plants.

Of course, what school year 2021–2022 will look like is already being discussed. Right now, we know distancing will be reduced to three feet, so our class sizes will go up. Multiples (twins and triplets) will be placed together in the same class, as they were this year, to minimize contacts for families. (*Oh boy.* I will most likely have a set of triplet boys, siblings of a former student.)

Dr. Lind reports that the remote learning will probably still have to be offered, as not all students will be vaccinated (as of right now, vaccinations are not open to children under sixteen, but that is expected to change by the summer). Masks will still be required. There will be no option of shared supplies or toys or books.

Keeping the students for a full day presents issues;

namely, how to manage the lunch/recess schedule with distancing in place (some unlucky class will need to go to lunch at 10:30 a.m., making for a really long afternoon). How will we keep kids distanced—and masked—while on the playground?

Ultimately, I think the way our school district handled the pandemic situation this past year is admirable. Our plan was well-thought-out and well-executed. Being a smaller district, we were able to do what was best for the kids: the majority together, in school, for the majority of the year. Kindergarten students have been in person for 70% of their days in attendance.

I believe we were a model for other districts in this year of COVID-19. I am proud of us, proud of how we pulled together despite the incredible odds and made it happen. My thoughts turn back to a presentation our assistant principal, Kari Gedville, made at our Welcome Back Staff meeting last August. She shared a most moving blog post by Dr. Bevin Reinen, founder of Teach. Train. Love:

"Maybe, just maybe, we *are* prepared for this, at least much more than we realize.

Maybe *you* are prepared for this.